I WONDER Why

Pirates
Wore Earrings

and other questions
about piracy

Pat Jacobs

KINGFISHER
NEW YORK

KINGFISHER
LONDON & NEW YORK

Copyright © Kingfisher 2012
Published in the United States by Kingfisher,
175 Fifth Ave., New York, NY 10010
Kingfisher is an imprint of Macmillan Children's Books,
London.

Distributed in the U.S. and Canada by Macmillan,
175 Fifth Ave., New York, NY 10010

Library of Congress Cataloging-in-Publication data has been
applied for.

ISBN:978-0-7534-6791-6

Kingfisher books are available for special promotions and
premiums. For details contact: Special Markets Department,
Macmillan, 175 Fifth Ave., New York, NY 10010.

For more information, please visit www.kingfisherbooks.com
Printed in China
9 8 7 6 5 4 3 2 1
1TR/0612/UTD/WKT/140MA

Illustrations: Mark Bergin 12–13 (ship); Jean-Michel Girard
(The Art Agency) 25br, 30–31; Phil Jacobs 6–7 (map), 14, 17br;
Claudia Saraceni (The Art Agency) 4–5, 7br, 8–9, 10–11, 13tr,
13br, 15br, 19, 20–21, 22–23, 24, 25tr, 28–29; all cartoons: Peter
Wilks (Plum Pudding).

CONTENTS

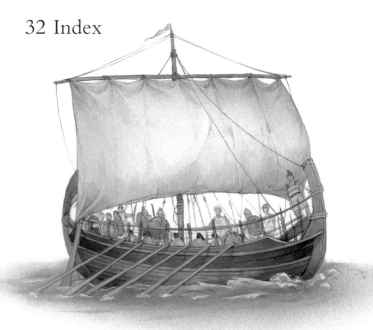

What is a pirate?

At sea, a pirate is a robber who travels by boat. Unlike the swashbuckling adventurers seen in movies, most pirates from the past led harsh, miserable lives aboard overcrowded ships. They suffered horrible injuries and diseases.

According to an ancient Greek myth, when the god Dionysus was kidnapped by pirates, he transformed himself into a lion. The pirates jumped overboard and were turned into dolphins.

Who were the first pirates?

Pirates have been roaming the seas ever since goods were first carried by boat. In the second century B.C., Cilicia, in what is now Turkey, became a center for pirates. These sea raiders ambushed ships and kidnapped people for ransom or to sell as slaves.

Who were the Sea Peoples?

Pirates usually attacked other ships, but some, such as the mysterious Sea Peoples, raided towns as well. These tribes first invaded Egypt in about 1220 B.C. For almost one hundred years they were the most feared sea raiders in the Mediterranean region.

Roman emperor Julius Caesar was captured by Cilician pirates who demanded a ransom of 20 talents (gold pieces). Caesar was insulted and insisted he was worth more, so they raised the price.

The Sea Peoples were defeated by Pharaoh Ramesses III in about 1178 B.C. He lined the banks of the Nile with archers, who fired at the pirates' ships when they tried to land.

Where did pirates go pirating?

Pirates were found wherever there was something to steal. In ancient times, sea raiders roamed the Mediterranean and Vikings plundered north European countries. Later, powerful pirate fleets terrorized the Asian seas and the Caribbean region became a pirate hot spot.

The Vikings have a reputation for being dirty, wild-haired savages, but compared to their neighbors they were unusually clean. They bathed every Saturday and regularly combed their hair.

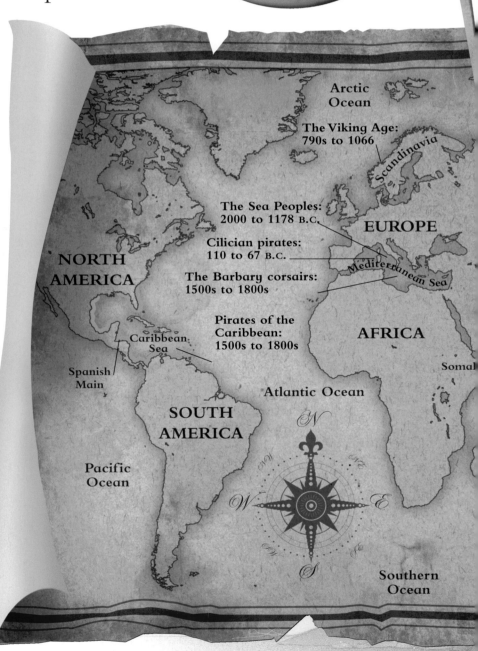

Arctic Ocean

The Viking Age: 790s to 1066

Scandinavia

The Sea Peoples: 2000 to 1178 B.C.

EUROPE

Cilician pirates: 110 to 67 B.C.

The Barbary corsairs: 1500s to 1800s

Mediterranean Sea

NORTH AMERICA

Pirates of the Caribbean: 1500s to 1800s

AFRICA

Caribbean Sea

Spanish Main

Somal

Atlantic Ocean

SOUTH AMERICA

Pacific Ocean

Southern Ocean

Which pirate pair were famous for their beards?

The Barbarossa (red beard) brothers were Barbary corsairs. These pirates, based in North Africa, captured people from Europe to sell as slaves.

Were Vikings pirates?

The Vikings were Scandinavian explorers, warriors, and traders. They looted villages and monasteries between the 700s and the 1000s, when trade and piracy went hand in hand.

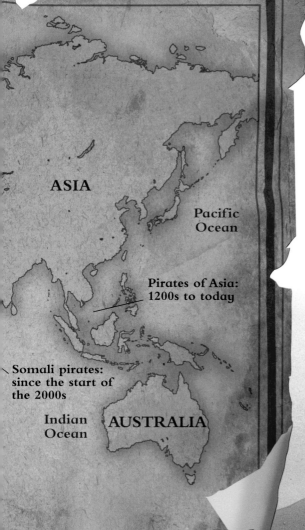

ASIA

Pacific Ocean

Pirates of Asia: 1200s to today

Somali pirates: since the start of the 2000s

Indian Ocean

AUSTRALIA

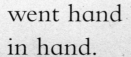

Did pirates have a golden age?

Calico Jack (1682–1720), known for his colorful clothing, was a pirate captain who attacked ships in the Caribbean.

Pirate activity grew between the 1600s and 1700s. This is often known as the "golden age" of piracy. During this time, treasure ships traveling to Spain from the Spanish Main (see page 6) regularly came under attack by both pirates and privateers.

Privateer Henry Morgan dressed hollowed-out logs, filled with explosives, to look like a pirate crew. He sailed this "fire ship" into a Spanish flagship and destroyed it.

Who was the most successful pirate?

Bartholomew Roberts (1682–1722), known as Black Bart, was the last great pirate of the golden age. He captured 470 ships and had such a fierce reputation that most crews surrendered to him without a fight.

What was a privateer?

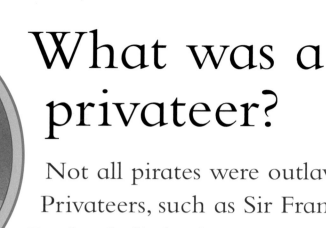

Not all pirates were outlaws. Privateers, such as Sir Francis Drake (left), had permission from their government to attack and rob enemy ships during wartime.

After fruitless months at sea, buccaneer Pierre Le Grand cut a hole in the side of his own ship to force his crew to board a Spanish galleon in search of booty.

Who were the buccaneers?

Buccaneers attacked Spanish ships in the Caribbean during the 1600s. They struck at high speed, taking their victims by surprise. They were named after the barbecues, known as "boucans," they used to smoke meat.

How did people become pirates?

Some people willingly joined a pirate crew to escape harsh lives on shore. Others were forced to become pirates when their ships were captured. Naval seamen sometimes chose to jump ship, tempted by a share of the pirates' booty.

A captured seaman was often offered the choice of signing the pirate code (see page 23) or being executed.

What was the worst job onboard?

Manning the bilge pump was such a horrible job it was often used as a punishment. The bilge is a space at the bottom of the hull where seawater collects when it seeps into a ship. This foul-smelling water has to be pumped out, otherwise it would rot the wood.

Musicians were popular aboard a ship because they kept the crew entertained. They also played very loudly before and during battles to scare the pirates' victims.

What made a good captain?

A successful captain made sure that there was always plenty of booty to share among the crew. Whenever he went ashore, he gathered information about valuable cargoes, so the pirates were ready to strike when their victims set sail.

Scottish slave Red Legs Greaves stowed away on a pirate ship by mistake and was forced to become a pirate. He was known as "Red Legs" because he wore a kilt and his legs got burned in the Caribbean sun.

What types of ships did pirates have?

Pirates needed fast ships so they could catch their prey and outrun the pirate hunters. The ideal ship was well-armed and sturdy enough to survive a raging storm, but pirates often had to make do with any vessel they could steal.

Crow's nest

Wealthy sugar planter Stede Bonnet was an unlikely and very unsuccessful pirate. He bought his ship, instead of stealing it, and paid his crew from his own pocket.

Rudder

Keel

1	Captain's cabin	6	Gundeck
2	Food store	7	Bilgewater pumps
3	Bilges (where dirty water collects)	8	Forecastle
4	Quarterdeck	9	Galley (ship's kitchen)
5	Capstan (for winding rope)	10	Shot locker (ammunition store)

How did pirates find their way?

The navigator was one of the most important members of the crew. He used a sextant to measure the angle of the sun or the stars, and a compass to guide the ship in the correct direction.

Bowsprit

Anchor

Pirates often flew an enemy's flag so they could get close to their victim's ship. At the last minute, they switched the flag for their own.

Did pirates take care of their ships?

Every few months, pirates had to take their ships out of the water to scrape off the barnacles that slowed them down. This was called careening. It was a very dangerous time for the crew, as they had no way to escape attack.

What was the Jolly Roger?

The Jolly Roger was a flag flown on pirates' ships. Often, just the sight of it was enough to make their victims surrender. Most pirates flew the skull and crossbones, but some had their own fearsome designs, as shown below.

Black Bart's flag

Blackbeard's flag

Christopher Moody's flag

Henry Avery's flag

Calico Jack's flag

Thomas Tew's flag

Pirates sometimes threw stink bombs filled with foul-smelling liquid on board ships to make their victims surrender. Or they dropped them below deck to drive the crew out of their cabins.

What weapons did pirates have?

Pirates used all kinds of cutthroat weapons, including axes, daggers, and cutlasses, as well as muskets and pistols. Most pistols only fired one shot, so pirates would hang several loaded guns from ribbons around their necks.

Sailors often walked barefoot, so pirates tossed caltrop (four-pointed spikes) on deck to pierce their victims' feet.

How did pirates attack?

Although pirates often had cannon and other heavy weapons, they did not want to risk sinking their victims' ships before they could plunder them. They preferred to swarm on board, using grappling hooks and ropes to scale the sides of the ship, and fight the crew hand to hand.

What cargo did pirates steal?

As well as gold, silver, jewels, and money, pirates took everyday things such as food and clothes. Tools, weapons, and ammunition were seized, too. Pirates even took their victims' ships, especially if they were bigger and better than their own.

Pirates often stole maps showing ships' trade routes across the sea, so they knew just where to lie in wait for their next victims.

Did pirates bury their treasure?

Most pirates divided their booty among the crew according to their rank, then they sold it and spent the money. One of the few pirates known to have buried his hoard is William Kidd (c.1645–1701), who hid his loot on Gardiner's Island near New York.

What was the most valuable booty?

One of the most prized treasures was a ship's medicine chest. This contained herbs and roots, which were mixed to make medicines, and equipment such as knives, saws, syringes, and grippers for pulling teeth. Blackbeard once held a group of wealthy citizens hostage until the town handed over a chest full of medicines.

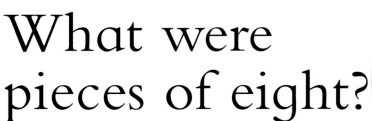

What were pieces of eight?

Pieces of eight were Spanish coins made of silver. Each was worth eight reales (smaller coins) and could be cut into eight pieces. They were used all around the world. The ships that transported them were often attacked by pirates.

What did pirates do to their captives?

Pirates often tried to persuade their victims to join them, especially those with special skills, such as doctors or carpenters. The Barbary corsairs sold their captives as slaves. Slave ships were very popular targets for the pirates of the Caribbean, because their human cargo was so valuable.

Cruel pirate captain Edward Low cut off the ears of one of his captives. Then, Low sprinkled them with salt and fed them to him.

Keelhauling was a common punishment aboard pirate ships. The victim was tied to a rope and dragged along the bottom-most part of the ship, called the keel, so that the barnacles scraped his skin.

18

Did prisoners have to walk the plank?

When the Dutch ship *Vhan Fredericka* was captured, in 1829, its crew were made to walk along a plank, hung over the edge of the ship, with cannon balls tied to their feet, and forced to jump into the sea. In most cases, though, pirates just shot their victims or threw them overboard.

How did pirates punish each other?

A bad captain, or a crew member who broke the pirate code (see page 23), was often marooned on an uninhabited island with nothing but a pistol and a few days' water. Few survived, and many shot themselves to avoid a slow death.

What was a pirate meal like?

Keeping food fresh was impossible on board a ship. After a week or two, pirates were reduced to eating salted meat, which was often crawling with maggots, and "hardtack" biscuits full of weevils (tiny beetles).

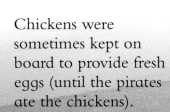

Chickens were sometimes kept on board to provide fresh eggs (until the pirates ate the chickens).

Why did pirates have rotten teeth?

Pirates soon ran out of fresh fruit and vegetables, so many suffered from scurvy—a disease caused by a lack of vitamin C. It made their teeth fall out, their skin turn pale and rough, and their legs very fat.

Did pirates have wooden legs?

Pirates' wounds often became infected. Then their only chance of survival was to have the injured limb sawn off by the ship's surgeon or carpenter. Most died from loss of blood, but some, including 16th-century French privateer François Le Clerc, survived. He became known as "Jambe de Bois," meaning leg of wood.

In 1670, Sir Henry Morgan's crew were so hungry they had to eat their leather satchels for dinner.

Did pirates have parrots?

British pirates returning from the tropics sometimes brought parrots back because they fetched a good price in London, but they did not usually keep them as pets.

Why did pirates wear earrings?

Seamen believed that piercing their ears with precious metals would improve their eyesight, and good sight was essential for spotting likely victims— and pirate hunters.

Stowaways on pirate ships included rats, fleas, spiders, and scorpions. Rats made themselves at home in the food store and often ate better than the pirates did.

Why did pirate ships smell so bad?

Water was a luxury at sea, so pirates did not wash or change their clothes for weeks—or even months. The smell of unwashed bodies, combined with rotting meat and filthy bilgewater, soon spread throughout the ship.

Did pirates have rules?

The pirate code usually included rules about sharing booty and payment for injuries. Pirates were paid for the loss of limbs and other parts of their bodies, according to the code. Black Bart's code included the rule that lights and candles must be put out at eight o'clock.

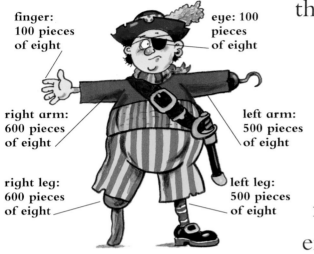

finger:
100 pieces
of eight

eye: 100
pieces
of eight

right arm:
600 pieces
of eight

left arm:
500 pieces
of eight

right leg:
600 pieces
of eight

left leg:
500 pieces
of eight

Where did pirates sell their loot?

When pirates had booty to sell, they would head for a pirate haven. These were refuges, safe from pirate hunters, where pirates were free to trade their stolen goods, spend their money, and repair their ships.

Port Royal, Jamaica, was a famous pirate stronghold.

Who was Blackbeard?

Blackbeard was a cunning and fearless English pirate, named Edward Teach (c.1680–1718). He put burning ropes under his hat before an attack. Slings of pistols, knives, and cutlasses also added to his fearsome appearance.

Blackbeard ambushed ships in the Caribbean and along the east coast of North America in the 1700s.

Why did Blackbeard lose his head?

Blackbeard's last battle took place in 1718, when he came face to face with naval lieutenant Robert Maynard (c.1684–1751). Blackbeard suffered many sword and gunshot wounds before falling down dead. His head was cut off and hung from the bow of Maynard's ship as a warning to other pirates.

Although Blackbeard struck fear into most seamen, he was very popular with women. During his short life, he had more than 12 wives.

What happened to the *Queen Anne's Revenge*?

Blackbeard's famous flagship ran aground near North Carolina. The wreck was discovered in 1996. Since then, thousands of objects, including a collection of terrifying weapons, have been recovered.

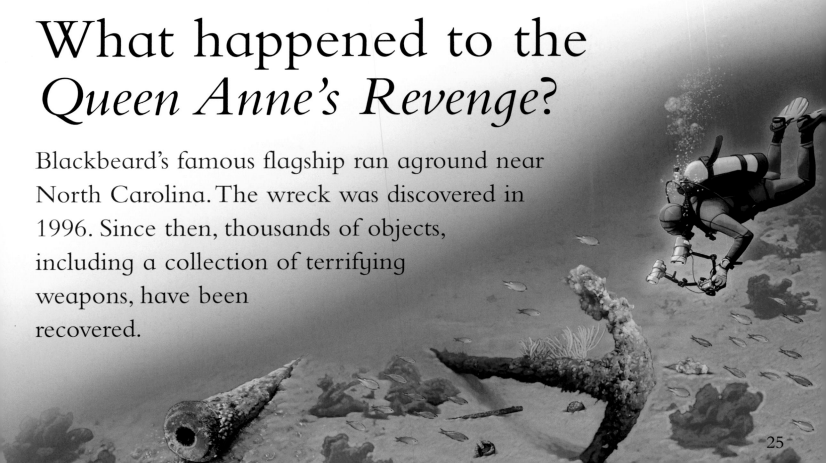

Could women be pirates?

Anne Bonny (1702–1782) and Mary Read (c.1690–1721) disguised themselves as men to serve aboard Calico Jack's ship. They were captured but escaped hanging because they were expecting babies.

Sadie Farrell was an American river pirate. She was nicknamed Sadie the Goat because she would headbutt her victims in the stomach.

Were babies born at sea?

Grace O'Malley was an Irish chieftain and fearless pirate in the 1500s. It is said that she gave birth at sea, and defended her ship against Turkish attackers the very next day.

After a storm, American pirate Rachel Wall (1760–1789) would stand on deck and scream for help. When a ship came to her aid, her husband and his crew would take their valuables and sink the ship with all onboard.

Were female pirates as fearsome as men?

Ruthless Madame Cheng (also called Ching Shih) terrorized the China Sea in the 1800s. She commanded about 80,000 pirates. If any of them deserted (ran away from duty), she would cut off their ears.

Who were the pirate hunters?

Pirates were pursued by naval ships and by other pirates or privateers who had become pirate hunters. Woodes Rogers was a famous pirate hunter who did battle with the pirates of the Caribbean. He offered the King's pardon to those who surrendered. Those who did not were soon captured.

Woodes Rogers (c. 1679–1732) was an English privateer who became a successful pirate hunter.

How were pirates punished?

The usual punishment for piracy was hanging, and few pirates who were captured escaped the noose. In 1573, the famous German pirate Klaus Hanslein and his crew were beheaded. Their heads were stuck on a row of stakes as a warning to others.

William Kidd was a pirate hunter who became an unlucky pirate. He only captured one ship, but he was hanged twice. The first time the British tried to hang him, the rope broke.

The bodies of William Kidd, Charles Vane (c.1680–1721), and Calico Jack were hung from gibbets.

What were the warnings against piracy?

The bodies of famous pirate captains were sometimes coated in tar and enclosed in an iron cage. This was hung from a wooden post, called a gibbet, for up to two years. This was done to remind people of the consequences of piracy.

Do pirates exist today?

There are fewer pirates now than during the golden age, but robbery on the high seas has not disappeared. Somalia, in Africa, and Indonesia are two of today's pirate hot spots. Modern pirates attack hundreds of ships every year. They often climb on board using ropes and grappling hooks, the same way that pirates did in times past.

Who do they attack?

Today's pirates usually live on shore, instead of spending their lives at sea. They use fast speedboats to attack tankers and cargo ships sailing close to the coast, or they target smaller fishing boats and tourist yachts.

Not all pirates use boats. Some, armed with only a computer, produce pirate DVDs or computer software, by making illegal copies.

Pirates demand huge sums of money for the return of valuable cargo. They often ask for it to be dropped on deck, but a ransom of $13 million, which was paid for the release of an oil tanker, weighs the same as a baby elephant.

What do today's pirates steal?

It can be difficult for pirates to sell large quantities of oil or other cargo. Instead, they steal electronic equipment, cash, and other valuables. Often, like the Cilician pirates who kidnapped Julius Caesar more than 2,000 years ago, they capture people or ships and demand a ransom for their return.

Index